The Legend of Sleepy Hollow

Retold by Robert D. San Souci

Illustrated by Daniel San Souci

Doubleday & Company, Inc., Garden City, New York

For my godchild, Andrea,
and my nephew, Mark
—Bob

For Bob Ribelin
—Dan

Designed by Virginia M. Soulé

Library of Congress Catalog Card Number 86-2064

Text copyright © 1986 by Doubleday & Company, Inc.
Illustrations copyright © 1986 by Daniel San Souci

Library of Congress Cataloging-in-Publication Data

San Souci, Robert.
    The legend of Sleepy Hollow.

    Summary: A superstitious schoolmaster, rival for the
hand of a wealthy farmer's daughter, has a terrifying
encounter with a headless horseman.
    [1. New York (State)—Fiction.   2. Ghosts—Fiction]
I. San Souci, Daniel, ill.   II. Irving, Washington,
1783–1859.   Legend of Sleepy Hollow.   III. Title.
PZ7.S1947Le   1986   [Fic]
ISBN 0–385–23396–5
ISBN 0–385–23397–3 (lib. ed.)

In a cove on the eastern shore of the Hudson River lies the village of Tarry Town. Some two miles away is a little valley among high hills, which is one of the quietest places in the whole world. A small brook glides through it with just murmur enough to lull one to sleep; and the occasional whistle of a quail, or tapping of a woodpecker, is perhaps the only sound that breaks the stillness.

This hidden glen is known as Sleepy Hollow. A drowsy, dreamy feeling hangs over the place. Some say an old Indian medicine man made magic there long ago. Certainly the place casts a spell over the minds of the people who live there.

The entire valley abounds with local tales, haunted spots, and twilight superstitions. Here stars shoot and meteors glare more often than in any other part of the country, and sleepers are frequently troubled by nightmares.

Many ghosts are said to haunt this enchanted region—and the best known of these is a headless man on horseback. He is reported to be the ghost of a soldier of the Revolutionary War, whose head was carried away by a cannonball in some battle or other. Frightened travelers often see him hurrying along in the gloom of night, on the wings of the wind.

He is known, at all country firesides, as the Headless Horseman of Sleepy Hollow.

In an early period of American history, a man named Ichabod Crane came to live in Sleepy Hollow, as schoolmaster for the children of the glen.

The name Crane fit him very well. He was tall, but exceedingly skinny, with narrow shoulders, long arms and legs, hands that dangled far beyond his sleeves, and feet as big as shovels. His head was small, and flat on top, with huge ears, large green glassy eyes, and a long nose. Striding along on a windy day, his clothes fluttering about him, he looked like a scarecrow escaped from a cornfield.

His schoolhouse was a low building of one large room that stood in a lonely but pleasant place, just at the foot of a woody hill. A huge birch tree gave it shade, and a brook ran alongside.

Because teaching paid him just enough to live on and no more, he picked up extra coins working as a singing master, instructing young folk in voice and music.

But for all his practical side, Ichabod Crane loved stories of monsters and marvels; and living in the spellbound region of Sleepy Hollow increased his interest in such stories. Often, after he dismissed his class in the afternoon, he stretched himself out on the clover bordering the little stream by his schoolhouse. Then he would read frightful tales, until the gathering dusk made reading impossible.

Afterward, as he returned through the woods to the farmhouse where he was staying, every sound excited his imagination. The moan of the whippoorwill, the boding cry of the tree toad, the dreary hooting of the screech owl—all made him think of ghosts and evil spirits.

Ichabod also took fearful pleasure in spending long winter evenings with the old country wives as they sat spinning by the fire, while a row of apples roasted along the hearth. He listened eagerly to their tales of ghosts and goblins; of haunted fields, brooks, bridges, and houses; and particularly of the Headless Horseman of Sleepy Hollow.

But the very stories that brought him pleasure in snug rooms filled with the cozy glow of a crackling wood fire brought him terror on his walk home.

What fearful shapes and shadows he saw in the dim and ghastly glare of a snowy night! How he was startled by a bush covered with snow that looked like a sheeted ghost! How a blast of wind, howling among the trees, made him think the Headless Horseman was galloping by!

These terrors of the night vanished at daybreak, when Ichabod gave his thoughts to other matters—especially to Katrina Van Tassel. She was the only child of old Baltus Van Tassel, the richest farmer in the neighborhood. She was a blooming young woman of eighteen: plump as a partridge, ripe and rosy-cheeked as one of her father's peaches, and famed as much for her beauty as for the rich farmlands she would one day own.

When Ichabod visited Van Tassel's farm to give Katrina her singing lesson, he would often pause and roll his eye over the fertile meadows; the rich fields of grain and Indian corn; and the orchard burdened with ruddy fruit, which surrounded the farmhouse. At such moments, he vowed to try even harder to win the affections of the beautiful Katrina.

But Katrina had many admirers, and the foremost among them was a burly, roaring young man, Brom Van Brunt. He was handsome, in a rough sort of way, and good-humored by and large—although he was always ready for a good fight. In fact, his strength gained him the nickname Brom Bones, because he had cracked a good number in his day.

Ichabod knew that to challenge such a rival would be mad, so he made extra visits to the farmhouse to instruct Katrina in her singing, chat with her father, and place himself in favor with them both.

Brom would have preferred a good clean fight, and he boasted to his gang of roughriders, "I'll fold the schoolmaster in half and tuck him on a shelf in his own schoolhouse."

But Ichabod was far too careful to give him the chance. So Brom and his friends began playing awful tricks: smoking out Ichabod's singing class by stopping up the chimney; breaking into the schoolhouse at night and turning everything topsy-turvy, so that poor Ichabod thought witches had made mischief; even training Van Tassel's dog to whine when Ichabod gave Katrina a singing lesson.

Matters went on like this for quite some time.

One fine autumn afternoon, while Ichabod was reading to his class, a servant of old Van Tassel's knocked on the schoolhouse door.

"Yes, my good fellow?" said Ichabod, peering down his long nose at the man.

"My master invites you to make merry with him at a quilting frolic this evening."

"Ah!" said Ichabod, delighted, sure that this was a sign of increased favor with the Van Tassel family. "And did Miss Katrina send a private message to me at the same time?"

"No, sir. Should she have?" asked the puzzled servant.

"Never mind, never mind," said Ichabod impatiently, shooing the man out the door.

Then he hurried through the day's lessons and dismissed class an hour early. He rushed back to his room to brush his best (and only) blue suit and arrange his thin hair by a bit of broken mirror.

He borrowed his landlord's horse for the evening: a broken-down plow horse, whose mane and tail were tangled and knotted with burrs. Still, old and sad as he looked, there was some fire left in the animal, which was why he was named Gunpowder.

Ichabod rode with short stirrups, which brought his knees nearly up to the pommel of the saddle; his sharp elbows stuck out like a grasshopper's; he carried his whip in his hand like a royal scepter. A small wool hat rested on top of his nose, because his forehead was so narrow, and the skirts of his blue coat fluttered out almost to Gunpowder's tail. As his horse jogged along, the motion of Ichabod's arms was like the flapping of a pair of wings.

Still, in his mind, he saw himself as a valiant knight on a noble steed.

"Tonight," he announced to Gunpowder, "I am going to ask for the delicate little dimpled hand of Katrina."

Gunpowder merely neighed.

It was early evening when Ichabod arrived at the Van Tassel farmhouse, which he found filled with neighbors from far and near.

His arrival was overshadowed, however, by the arrival of Brom Bones. A famed horseman, Brom galloped up on his steed, Daredevil, a creature full of mischief, just like his master. Daredevil kicked up a cloud of dust that settled over Ichabod and his mount.

Brushing himself off, Ichabod followed Brom to the door, where both were greeted by smiling old Baltus Van Tassel, who invited them to come in and help themselves.

This they did, quickly finding separate corners. Ichabod soothed his injured pride with wonderful food and drink—all the time casting anxious eyes in the direction of Katrina, who had been drawn into a private talk with Brom.

But Ichabod, who prided himself on his dancing as much as his singing, took heart when music from the common room, or hall, summoned all to dance. Brom Bones, he knew, was no dancer. And Katrina loved to dance. So Ichabod invited her to be his partner, and she delightedly accepted.

They danced and laughed and caused no end of amused comments from other couples around them. Brom Bones, bursting with love and jealousy, sat brooding by himself all the while.

When the music ended, most folk gathered in a corner of the room, talking about ghosts and goblins and all the other creatures that haunted Sleepy Hollow. Inevitably, most stories were about the Headless Horseman, who had been heard several times recently, patrolling the countryside after dark.

Brom Bones told the most exciting tale.

"One night," he began, "while riding through the Hollow, I found I was being followed by the midnight soldier, who tried to ride me down."

"What happened then, dear Brom?" asked Katrina, hand at her throat.

"Why, Daredevil beat the goblin horse with ease," boasted Brom. "We were two lengths ahead in the race by the time we reached the old church bridge. The ghostly horse would not set hoof on it."

"What about the Horseman himself?" asked Ichabod, his own hand at his long throat. He had quite forgotten his rivalry with Brom in his eagerness to hear every detail of the man's story.

"Horse and rider vanished in a flash of fire, just as I reached the far side of the bridge," Brom replied.

"The ghost won't cross the old church bridge," said Ichabod thoughtfully. "I will remember that."

Shortly afterward, the party gradually broke up as neighbors left on horseback or with their families in wagons.

Brom rode off on Daredevil, but Ichabod lingered on to have a private talk with Katrina.

When he was able to draw her aside from the last few guests, he pressed her hand and said, "Dear, *dear* Katrina, I must share the feeling I have for you."

Katrina smiled, not having heard Ichabod's words over the shouted good-byes of several rather loud cousins.

"If you'll only say the word, I'll ask your father for your hand this very night."

To Ichabod's dismay, Katrina burst out laughing. When she had wiped away tears of merriment, she said, "Dear song master, you catch me by surprise. I am not at all ready to think about marriage." Another fit of giggles shook her, then she added, "You may continue to teach me singing—but only if you don't bring up this foolishness again."

Then she excused herself to help direct the servants in cleaning up, since Ichabod was now the only guest remaining.

Heavy-hearted, Ichabod left and mounted Gunpowder to start his lonely homeward journey, across the wooded hills that rise above Tarry Town.

It was the witching time of night, and all the stories of ghosts and goblins he had heard earlier—especially Brom's account of the Headless Horseman—now came crowding into his memory.

The night seemed to grow darker and darker; the moon and stars seemed to sink deeper in the sky; and driving clouds occasionally hid them from sight.

Ichabod had never felt so lonely and dismal.

As he entered the haunted woods, where so many of the ghostly stories had been set, his heart began to thump. He tried to sing to comfort himself, but found his throat too dry to make a sound.

He used his riding crop to urge his horse to a brisker trot; but the contrary old animal, instead of going forward, made a sudden sideways move into the brush.

Ichabod, whose fears increased with this delay, jerked on the reins and kicked the horse's flank. "Ho, Gunpowder! Giddup!" he rasped.

All in vain: Gunpowder lunged suddenly to the opposite side of the road and into a bramble thicket.

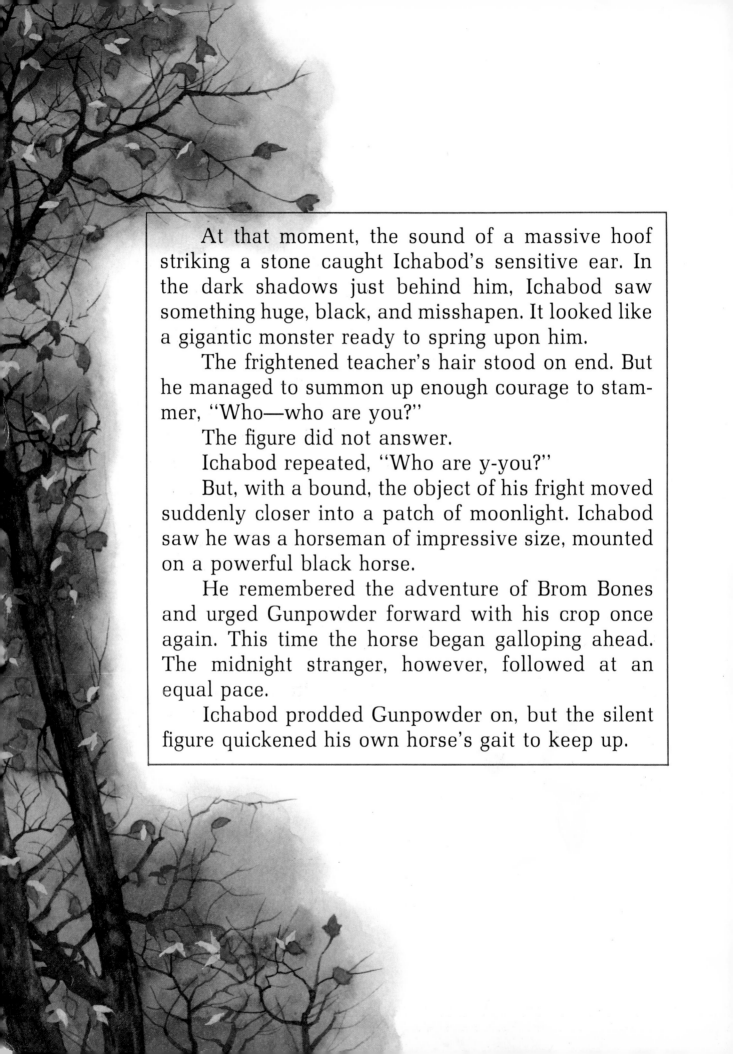

At that moment, the sound of a massive hoof striking a stone caught Ichabod's sensitive ear. In the dark shadows just behind him, Ichabod saw something huge, black, and misshapen. It looked like a gigantic monster ready to spring upon him.

The frightened teacher's hair stood on end. But he managed to summon up enough courage to stammer, "Who—who are you?"

The figure did not answer.

Ichabod repeated, "Who are y-you?"

But, with a bound, the object of his fright moved suddenly closer into a patch of moonlight. Ichabod saw he was a horseman of impressive size, mounted on a powerful black horse.

He remembered the adventure of Brom Bones and urged Gunpowder forward with his crop once again. This time the horse began galloping ahead. The midnight stranger, however, followed at an equal pace.

Ichabod prodded Gunpowder on, but the silent figure quickened his own horse's gait to keep up.

"Fly, Gunpowder!" yelled the schoolmaster, no longer able to control his fear. His shout so startled the horse that Gunpowder surged ahead with a clatter of hoofbeats.

Behind, their pursuers matched them, hoofbeats falling like a military march on the stony road.

When they galloped over a hilltop, Ichabod dared to look back. As he did, the figure behind was framed against the sky. Horror-struck, Ichabod saw that the gigantic figure, muffled in a cloak, was headless! His terror reached beyond all bounds when he saw that the head was carried before the rider on the pommel of his saddle. In the moonlight, to Ichabod's mind, the ghastly pale head looked as swollen and orange and leering as a jack-o'-lantern.

Ichabod rained a desperate shower of kicks and blows upon Gunpowder, and away they dashed. Stones flew and sparks flashed at every bound. Ichabod's thin coat fluttered in the air as he stretched his long, thin body away over his horse's head in his eagerness to escape the ghost.

They soon reached the road that turned out of Sleepy Hollow; but Gunpowder, who seemed possessed by a demon himself, suddenly made a wrong turn and plunged headlong downhill in the opposite direction. After a screech of terror, Ichabod realized there was still hope: they were now headed toward the old church bridge, and safety.

His steed's panic had kept Ichabod a hair's length ahead of his pursuer, but as they galloped into the shadow of the trees again, he felt the girths of his saddle give way. Then it began slipping from under him. He tried to hold it in place, but finally he had all he could do to save himself by clasping old Gunpowder around the neck while the saddle fell to the ground. A moment later, he heard it trampled underhoof by the dark horseman.

Ichabod, sometimes slipping to one side, sometimes to the other, and sometimes jolted painfully on the sharp ridge of his horse's backbone, could only hang on for dear life.

Then an opening in the trees showed the church bridge and the little whitewashed chapel beyond.

"That's where Brom Bones escaped the ghost!"

cried Ichabod. "If I can only cross that bridge, I'll be safe!"

He heard the black steed panting and snorting close behind him; he even thought he felt its hot breath blowing on him.

Ichabod gave a final kick, and old Gunpowder sprang onto the bridge, thundered over the planks, and gained the far side.

Only then did Ichabod look behind, expecting to see his pursuers vanish in a flash of fire.

Instead, he saw the Headless Horseman seated firmly in his saddle, hurling his head at Ichabod. As bright as the moon, as orange as a pumpkin, as swift as a shooting star, the awful thing sailed across the brook straight toward the terrified schoolmaster.

Ichabod tried to duck the horrible missile—but too late! It smacked into his own head with a tremendous *crash!*

He was tumbled backward into the dust, while Gunpowder bolted in one direction and the black steed and its goblin rider vanished in the opposite direction like a whirlwind.

The next morning, old Gunpowder was found, without his saddle, peacefully chewing grass at his master's gate.

Later, the children assembled for class at the schoolhouse, but the schoolmaster never showed up.

On the road leading to the old church bridge, people found the missing saddle trampled in the dirt. The tracks of horses' hooves—deeply gouged into the road, suggesting furious speed—were traced to the bridge. Just beyond, on the bank of the brook below the chapel, searchers found Ichabod's hat and, close beside it, a shattered pumpkin.

The stream was searched, but no trace of the schoolmaster was ever discovered.

This mysterious event caused much talk in Tarry Town for a long time.

An old farmer who visited New York several years later reported that Ichabod Crane was still alive, and had left the valley partly through fear of the ghost, and partly because of Katrina's rejection.

Shortly after his rival's disappearance, Brom Bones married Katrina. Whenever the story of Ichabod was related, he would wink; and he would always burst into laughter at the mention of the pumpkin found beside the brook. This led some to suspect that he knew more than he chose to tell.

Those old country wives, however, who are the best judges of these matters maintain to this day that Ichabod was carried off by the Headless Horseman. And the story remains a favorite one told in warm farm kitchens on cold winter evenings.